HOW TO BUILD A HEALTHY MOTHER-DAUGHTER RELATIONSHIP

PLAIN AND SIMPLE RECIPE FOR A LIFE-LONG

FRIENDSHIP WITH A GROWING-UP DAUGHTER

By Awatif Benchekor

Dedication

This book is lovingly dedicated as a token of appreciation to my beloved parents for whom I am so grateful...

Thank you for believing in me and teaching me the power of determination to strive for greatness, your unconditional love, unwavering support, and devotion have been the seed that made me grow and thrive...

I love you both.

Book Blurb

Are you struggling to build a close relationship with your daughter? Do you need a <u>roadmap</u> to create a secure and positive bond that defies the traditional **ONE-SIZE-FITS-ALL** approach to parenting a girl?

Well, this book has ALL the answers!

Whether you are looking to establish a new connection with your daughter or strengthen an existing one, this book will dive deep into understanding the dynamics of a strong mother-daughter relationship, from difficult stages and emotions to effective communication.

You will be provided with step-by-step strategies for developing trust and open communication you will learn simple yet effective Tips for navigating the challenges of a growing-up daughter during every stage of her life.

Plant the seed of a healthy connection today, and reap the benefit of an unbreakable bond with your daughter...

Table of Contents

Introduction

Have you been wondering how to interact with your daughter? Or what is the best way to connect with her? How can you ensure that she will grow up knowing how much you love her?

Everybody has a different childhood and relationship with their parents. Taking time to invest in a relationship with your daughter can be one of the most rewarding experiences in life.

So, how do you start?

Building a healthy relationship takes time, but it is worth it because it allows both people involved to grow closer together and, therefore, stronger.

Taking your time to build a strong and healthy relationship with your daughter is an investment that will pay off in the long run because it sets the foundation for her overall well-being, a positive relationship with her mother helps her feel secure and build self-esteem, both of which can lead to better behavior, academic success, and fewer emotional problems.

Additionally, a strong relationship provides trust and open communication which is important for navigating the adolescence years and beyond.

Ultimately the connection fostered in a healthy relationship, will last throughout a daughter's life and become the foundation of her most important relationships in life.

The love between a mother and daughter is unique. When your daughter becomes an adult, you may not be her priority, but what legacy are you leaving behind?

You may struggle to have a conversation with your daughter, but you can easily achieve it with the right tools and some patience. However, it's not always easy for a daughter to open up about her feelings or her life. So, you must make it a point to listen closely and observe her, so you know how she truly feels.

So, if you have a daughter and have struggled to create a great relationship with her, this book is for you, it will help shed some light on what's needed to build a strong connection.

This book is a guide on how to start and maintain a healthy, meaningful relationship with your daughter, it is written for parents who want to strengthen the bond they share with their daughter but may not know where to start.

It's a practical, easy-to-follow guide to help you strengthen your bond with your daughter, it lays out the steps in a straightforward manner, making it simple for any parent seeking to build a closer and healthy relationship with their daughter.

You will find helpful advice on how to be a good listener, establish open communication and engage in activities that both of you enjoy, as well as insights on how to be a positive influence and build trust, it will help you kickstart your relationship with your daughter and foster the lasting friendship.

It provides tips on how to create open dialogues, and handle disagreements as well as making the conversation process more enjoyable, it's a simple yet reliable roadmap to help you nurture a lasting and meaningful bond with your daughter.

Becoming a daughter's best friend can be one of the most incredible relationships in life. It depends on how you approach the situation and how diligent you are in building your connection with her, it takes commitment and patience. You must devote time and energy to this special relationship.

You need to show her how much you care about her more than anything else – including your own life. It's all about being everything she needs and could want from a mother figure in her life by taking the place of an older sister or close friend.

For this to work, you need to be more than just a mother; she needs constant nurturing and support that only a great friendship can give her. You must be a best friend in every sense of the word.

Spending quality time together, getting to know her more profoundly, and creating a solid emotional bond are all part of maintaining your relationship with your daughter.

So "Building a healthy relationship with your growing-up daughter" will help you create an everlasting bond for a lifetime friendship. Once you have this relationship, you will enjoy seeing her grow into a confident, intelligent, loving woman ready to face any issue or challenge in life.

Chapter 1

The Power of Love in a
Mother-Daughter Relationship

L ittle in this world compares to the love shared between mother and daughter. This bond is more robust than siblings, closer than friends, and stronger than any other relationship.

To keep this strong bond alive through all stages while creating a tremendous mother-daughter relationship that will last a lifetime, certain principles need to be upheld by both sides.

The bond between mother and daughter has many aspects, but the most important is willpower. It takes a particular type of love to raise a child and resolve to stick through the challenging parts.

By finding a way to make her laugh, even when she is struggling, you will have found a way to strengthen your bond.

Understanding the importance of love in a mother-daughter relationship

A mother's love for her child is not a choice; it's irrevocable. It's natural! This love knows no bounds, and there is no limit to what she will do for her daughter. To truly benefit from this love, you must understand its power and what it means for the future.

The importance of love in a mother-daughter relationship cannot be overstated. Your love for her will also increase as your daughter grows and matures. As your daughter ages from a toddler to a young woman, you will want to express your love to her. You will want to show her how much she means to you; you can do that by simply being constantly available and treating her with respect and kindness.

A mother-daughter relationship is one of the most relationships a daughter can have, and that means showing love and warmth are paramount, through providing love and affection, a mother can give her daughter the security and support she needs while she is growing and developing.

Furthermore, the bond between mother and daughter is the cornerstone of a daughter's self-esteem, setting an example of the kind of relationships she can expect to have with other people throughout her life, this understanding of love and connection is invaluable and cannot be understated.

You can share your love with your daughter in many ways: You can be her best friend, you can help her through hard times, and you can make sure that she feels safe, secure, and happy.

You will also realize that love is not only important in a mother-daughter relationship – It is crucial. Just as your daughter needs to be loved by you, she must learn how to express it herself. It will give her confidence and mold her into the best version of herself possible. she will find a peace that sets her up for success.

In short, it teaches girls to be fearless and strong, which is what they need to succeed in every area of their lives. More than anything, it will give them faith.

The same can be said for things like finding a hobby together. When raising your daughter, you will learn what she is made of. This is when the real work begins because you must help nurture her interests before they fade or get overshadowed by the world around her. You need to help cultivate her early so she can blossom into something extraordinary.

If you can be there for her now as her mother and make her feel secure, she will be able to carry that sense of security with her thought her life and be there for others when they need it.

As a mother, love your daughter unconditionally and without reservation – that means accepting her for who she is, no matter what. it means loving her for both the good and bad, for successes and failures. For the moments she shines and those she does not.

To love her unconditionally is to provide a safe and secure space where she can be and learn without fear of criticism or judgment. It's to accept her as she is and to give her the love and support, she needs to become the person she wants to be.

If you do this for her, you will see that your love is returned a thousandfold, and you will be able to create a strong bond that will last for years to come

Starting a family is a fantastic experience, but it is only made better by a mother's love. When you raise your child with love and compassion, you will make this bond unbreakable. Not only will your daughter be loyal to you and your family, but she will also fight to protect it.

Being their mother is one of the most extraordinary callings in life, and it is one that you should not take lightly. Your bond with your daughter is powerful and will be substantial regardless of the things that come along the way. She will always be your baby girl, and she will always love you. By doing this, you are showing her that there is nothing more significant than a mother's love, it's irreplaceable, and it's by no means the most precious gift your daughter can have during her lifetime.

Using love and logic to handle conflicts and challenges

Early childhood years are the most enjoyable and essential phase of life. The development of your daughter during these years lays a foundation for her life as an adult. She is curious to learn everything around her when she is a toddler. She wants to explore the world by using her sense organs - look, hear, touch, smell, and taste. She is just like a sponge that absorbs everything around it.

You can make your toddler develop into an intelligent and creative child by using your love and logic toward her.

First, start conversations by asking thoughtful questions. This will give your daughter an opportunity to express herself and be heard.

Communicate clearly and consistently. Set limits and expectations in a supportive and consistent manner.

Listen and respond with understanding. This will show your daughter that her feelings and experiences are valued.

Address misbehavior calmly and with a sense of understanding it is important to show your daughter that it is ok to make mistakes and that there are always better options.

Offer logical consequences. Give your daughter choices when misbehavior occurs and explain the consequences of each choice.

Use natural and logical consequences. Natural consequences are those that happen without any action on your part, and logical consequences are those that you guide your daughter to in order to help her learn and grow.

Praise good behavior. let your daughter know that you appreciate her effort and that her behavior is noticed and appreciated.

Remain patient and remain in control. This will help your daughter to learn about and develop healthy boundaries around her behavior.

As she grows into a child, she develops her judgment and reasoning skills.

It is never too early to build a strong bond with your daughter. Eventually, she grows into a beautiful, wise, virtuous, and confident woman.

By using love and logic to solve your toddler's problems or conflicts, she will learn to respect the world around her. You can also teach her how to love and be kind by using your logic to strengthen her character.

Let your daughter enjoy every moment of life so that she grows into a responsible person as an adult. She will realize the importance of responsibility in her preteen and teen years.

You can show your daughter that there is nothing more important than loving others; a true mother is always there for her, guides and cares for her equally - no matter what situation she is in.

You will tell her that there is nothing more important than this love - to love and be loved. It's, therefore, necessary to take every little challenge or conflict your daughter faces in her stride. Don't panic or get angry when your daughter approaches you with a problem. Use love and logic to help her deal with it.

Rearing your daughter right is not easy, but it's worth all the effort and hard work you put into it. Be the best mom for your daughter so you will reap benefits for years. Ultimately, she will love you and always want to be with you. Your daughter is not just your baby girl - she will be your family member and an essential part of your life.

A strong foundation of love and logic helps children build confidence in their lives. Effective communication between parents and children leads to better trust, which is generally the main ingredient for building confidence in life.

Love and logic help children take full responsibility for their actions. They learn how to communicate effectively with others and make mature choices in life. This can be utilized in a classroom as well as in general society.

Using love and logic helps children cope with anger and stress. It helps build self-confidence, as well as self-worth. Love and logic are powerful parenting tools that must be used effectively in raising a happy child.

So how do you use love and logic with your growing-up daughter to handle conflicts and challenges effectively?

Firstly, show her that you love her unconditionally.

Model positive responses to mistakes and failures. Show your daughter that mistakes and failures are an integral part of learning and don't need to be feared.

Encourage her to come up with her own solutions. Give her the tools and resources she needs to work through her problems and come up with her own solutions.

Give her real and meaningful responsibility. This will not only help her build confidence but also show her that you trust her and value her opinion.

Provide an encouraging environment. Encourage your daughter and provide a space where she feels safe to take risks and be creative.

Praise the successes. Celebrate her small victories and take the time to express your appreciation for her effort and hard work.

Connect with her interests and activities. Spend time learning about and engaging in the activities that she enjoys. This will help her see you as an ally and mentor.

The love and logic approach teaches kids to accept responsibility for their actions and emotions.

You need to understand that kids do not always see the long-term effects of their actions, so it may require further explanation on your part about why something was wrong.

There are times when your daughter may seem confused about why her action was improper and when you provide "logical consequences" she still doesn't get it. This is where your inner, loving parent comes in.

This inner-loving parent knows how to give kids the tools and strategies to help make sense of how best to approach situations. Make her understand that she can also talk to you about her frustrations and disappointments. Listen to how she feels, and most importantly, show that you've listened.

Establishing trust creates a secure bond that helps build confidence in your daughter's life. Learn how to communicate effectively. Always speak with love and kindness when negotiating. This will help her understand the reason behind your decisions.

Your role as a parent is to show what is best for her, so make logical choices when making decisions that affect both of you together.

While it's important to empathize with your daughter, it's equally important that you give some logical advice on how she can resolve the conflict or the challenge. Your main concern is your daughter's well-being and helping her be happy in life. Sometimes, it's best to keep advice simple and use examples to illustrate a point.

Love and logic are powerful parenting tools that can benefit parents and children. When used wisely and effectively, it can help build a strong and healthy relationship between mother and daughter leading to stronger bonds between them in the long run.

Chapter 2

Identifying and Addressing
Problematic Behaviors

It is not unusual to struggle with the problematic behaviors of your growing-up daughter. Mothers often express frustration about their daughter's seeming inability to control her temper, concentration, and impulse control. They report that their daughters present with behavior problems, but they are not sure what to do. They can be confused about what to do about adverse interactions with their daughter at school and in the community.

In the growing stages of a daughter's life, she is developing her identity, self-confidence, and independence. She is also making the transition from childhood to adolescence. This can bring forth some challenging behavior that may be difficult for a mother to cope with.

Although all children can choose what develops in their lives and how they deal with things, it might be wise to see if any problems or patterns emerge in your daughter's life at this critical time in her development and growth.

When she is a toddler or young child, she is not aware of the impact that her behavior can have on others. It is essential to start building good habits and patterns of behavior as early as possible in your daughter's life.

The goal in early childhood is to help your daughter learn healthy ways to interact with the people who are important to her. You can help her develop the skills and maturity to navigate the world and establish a loving relationship with herself and others.

The foundation on which she will build her life is being laid at this very young age. The earlier you can begin to shape and guide her behavior, the better she will be able to rely on herself and others as she matures into adulthood.

Problematic behavior is any behavior that affects the well-being of your daughter or others in her life in a way that does not support healthy relationships. When your daughter's behavior causes troubles to those around her, it is probably undesirable or inappropriate for her age. As a parent, you are concerned about what can be done to help your daughter develop into a well-adjusted person.

When your daughter is not using good judgment, you may feel that your approach to discipline and guidance is not working or that you are becoming ineffective. You might also feel embarrassed or upset when people question your ability as a parent of a difficult child. This can begin to affect the way that you view yourself and the way that you interact with those around you.

You may start to believe negative things about yourself as a parent and your daughter's abilities. You may begin to feel like a failure as a parent. You might also become discouraged or depressed, and overwhelmed if you cannot handle the situation.

Parents often find it difficult to teach their kids how to use self-control, discipline, and empathy when they are young. Fortunately, parents grow into adulthood with these skills.

Still, when your daughter is in high school or college, these skills may not be fully developed as she develops into an independent adult. As your preteen or teen daughter matures and continues through puberty, she will undergo developmental stages.

A difficult daughter comes with a package of trouble, including negative behavior, defiance, power struggles, blaming others, anger, and frustration. These characteristics can significantly affect any young girl's growth and development.

They emerge as your daughter tries to discover herself in this world and makes her way into adulthood step by step. She may become confused about what is expected from her and how she should behave as an adolescent female. She will go through trying and challenging times.

It is important to remember that your daughter's behavior is related to how she tries to make sense of the world and her daily experience in it. It is essential to know that your daughter's behavior has a purpose and a meaning, even though you may not always understand or agree with it.

A mother can learn to work patiently with her challenging daughter by gaining insight into how and why her behavior is emerging. Mothers need support to guide them in working with their daughters constructively for their growth and development without damaging the parent-child relationship.

Most of all, you as a mother need a clear plan with goals so that your daughter's behavior is more likely to improve rather than get worse. It is not always easy to know what to do when your growing-up daughter seems out of control or defiant. The key is to find a way to tell show her that you understand her. and help her learn new ways of dealing with situations. This recipe will give you practical strategies for solving day-to-day problems and working with your daughter toward positive change.

Understanding the reasons for constant conflicts with your daughter

Mothers have a unique bond with their daughters. When mothers and daughters are at odds, it can be incredibly stressful, frustrating, and challenging to resolve the problems that seem to be never-ending. The best way to handle these difficulties is to identify the specific behaviors that trouble you so that you can work as a team in which your daughter wants and needs to cooperate with you.

Most conflicts begin because either the daughter is doing something that she feels is natural for her (such as breaking curfew) or because there are misguided messages from peers or other adults that create conflict between her and her mother. Either way, these conflicts don't have to be a source of stress between mother and daughter. You can take steps to resolve issues in a calm, respectful manner. Stressful situations can be avoided if you and your daughter are willing to invest the time and effort needed to stay connected.

The reasons for constant conflicts between mother and daughter include:

1. Individual beliefs and different opinions of effective discipline.

Differences in beliefs, values, and opinions can lead to unresolved conflicts and ongoing disagreements. When belief systems are challenged, they create a conflict in what the mother and daughter believe to be right or wrong. Although your view of effective discipline may seem very different from your daughter's, this is inconsequential.

The issue is not different styles of discipline; instead, it is a difference in values (i.e., what's most important). Avoid threatening or using punishments without considering your child's needs. Instead, try to create a plan that offers family solutions and practical steps that you can use to make the right decisions.

2. Strengthening the mother-daughter bond despite unequal time commitment.

It's hard for mothers and daughters to make it together. Both of you need to set aside time to make plans together so that you can be a positive influence in your daughter's life. The more connected you are, the less likely she will have problems at school or with friends.

3. Differing perceptions about the consequences of actions

Mothers often do not understand their daughters' perspectives on particular situations. Instead of listening to your daughter's feelings and ideas, she may be hearing how you talk to her or the tone of your voice. This can prevent her from feeling supported or validated in her choices. Mother and daughter must work together to figure out the best communication methods.

4. Lack of communication

This is an essential reason for conflicts. The lack of communication between a mother and daughter can create feelings of resentments, hostility, and disconnection within the relationship.in order to overcome this conflict, it's important to prioritize time to have meaningful conversations and listen to each other, set aside time for fun activities, and build trust, try to create a healthy level of communication that brings you closer together.

5. Different needs and expectations

The mother-daughter relationship is a special bond that transcends everyday life and evolves over time as both individuals in the relationship grow and mature. With such an important relationship comes different expectations and needs that must be fulfilled in order to create a healthy and lasing bond. From the need of communication, respect, trust, and emotional support to the need for quality time spent together to ensure that both partners' expectations and needs are properly understood and met.

6. Boundary issues

Boundaries issues can be a challenge in a mother-daughter relationhip.it is important to recognize and respect the personal boundaries of each individual and to practice healthy communication and behavior to ensure that the mother and daughter can interact comfortably and respectfully. This means establishing clear guidelines and limits on behavior, as well as respecting each other's privacy and personal space. When boundary issues arise, it is important to address them promptly and constructively, as unresolved boundary issues can lead to conflict and distress in mother-daughter relationship.

7. Different family traditions and values

Family rules and traditions can often come to the surface leading to additional tension between the mother and the daughter. Some mothers have stringent rules that they expect their daughters to follow without exceptions, while others have more open or flexible rules based on their values or beliefs.

This can make it hard for your daughter to feel wholly secure or accepted. The best thing you can do is establish some rules and regulations that are realistic and within her capabilities, while remaining flexible enough to adapt to her changes. When she begins to understand that you aren't always going to be there to monitor every decision she makes, she will start accepting your family's boundaries and feeling more comfortable as a person.

Mothers and daughters must work together when conflicts arise instead of against each other. These recipes can help you set up good communication patterns to get what you need from the relationship. Don't let disagreements be a source of stress, but rather a platform to help you grow.

Although you may be tempted to blame your daughter for all her problematic behaviors, it would be more helpful to look deeper into why she is acting out. You must look at both sides and understand why it happens. To identify the causes, start by writing down problems that you and your daughter have been experiencing, including:

- Problems in school
- Problems with friends
- Problems with money and material possessions (for example, her spending or sharing)
- Problems with brothers and sisters
- Problems in the community (for example, at the mall or parties).

After you write down all these problems, go over them with someone objective and outside your family system - such as a counselor or supportive friend - to get their perspective on why you are having so many problems with your daughter.

Then make a list of all of your issues and possible reasons why they occur. By considering all aspects of the situation, you should be able to identify both the causes and the potential ways to resolve them. Also, be careful not to let your negative feelings about the situation take over and interfere with the possible solutions.

Identifying problematic behaviors and taking steps to address them

Identifying and managing your daughter's problematic behavior is a challenging yet rewarding process. As a parent, it's important to understand the dynamics of your daughter's behavior in order to properly intervene when needed. It is also important to look at the underlying causes of her behavior considering the emotional, Social, and environmental factors which may be influencing her decisions and actions. through establishing a strong foundation of communication and understanding, you can help to support your daughter as she navigates her way through the often complicated and overwhelming stages of growing up. As you begin to identify these problems and potential causes, you can then take steps to address them.

How do you identify problematic behaviors and take steps to address them?

To identify your daughter's problematic behavior, you should pay attention to her actions, words, and attitude. look for changes in her mood attitudes, and behavior such as increased irritability, acting out or withdrawing. All these can be signs of an underlying issue. Additionally, talking to your daughter's teachers and other adults who interact with her may help to better gauge her social situations and potential conflicts.

Once you identify the behavior, it is important to take steps to address it in a respectful, yet firm manner.

1. Identify how your daughter feels about everything that happens

Before you can determine what actions need to be taken, you must first understand your daughter's perspective on what is happening. You will gain this knowledge by talking to her and listening to her side of the story while maintaining objectivity. be sure to focus on the misbehavior rather than the individual and provide reinforcement when she displays the desired behavior.

2. Provide your daughter with a sense of security

Providing your daughter with a sense of security and safety is essential for her overall well-being. one way to do this is to sit with your daughter every day, talk and listen attentively to her and offer consistent support, love, and acceptance.

You can also encourage your daughter to participate in activities that she enjoys and provide her with a structure such as consistent routines. Finally, make sure to be available when your daughter needs you the most. In addition, you need to show her that she is important enough for you to invest time and energy into improving your relationship with her. This means showing interest in what she feels is essential while sharing insights into the world around her.

3. Don't fall into power struggles

When a problem arises between you and your daughter, it is essential not to get distracted by all the chaos going on during this time. Instead, try to focus on one problem at a time. Avoid all power struggles with your daughter by setting clear expectations and boundaries in a consistent and non-confrontational manner. Talk to your daughter about her feelings and explain to her what her expectations are in a calm and respectful manner.

When setting the limits, be consistent and clear with your expectations. Show your daughter that you are listening to her by acknowledging and responding to her concerns, even if you don't agree. respect her interests, beliefs and opinions. avoid using negative language and be fair and consistent when enforcing consequences for her behavior.

4. Accept her as she is now

If you can give your daughter the acceptance and trust that she needs to feel secure and comfortable whenever there is a conflict or problem between you two, you will start to see good results from the relationship. Your daughter will begin to feel the love and acceptance you give her and will no longer feel threatened or rejected by you. This allows her to be more open with you and honest about how she feels and perceives the world around her.

5. Listen to your daughter

Listen to your daughter is a key component of resolving problematic issues, being attentive and compassionate listener can help you identify any problematic behaviors causing distress and allow you to respond constructively. You should strive to listen with an open mind and be aware of your own feeling and expectations. try to understand the difference between her true intentions and the actions that she chooses. Ask her how she thinks that you can help her if she is facing a discomfort.

6. Give your daughter some privacy

When it comes to raising a daughter, it is important to provide her with an appropriate level of privacy. Giving her the necessary space to be herself and express her thoughts and feelings without the pressure of being scrutinized allows her to develop confidence and independence. It also helps teach her how to respect other people's privacy, as well as her own.

Offering your daughter some privacy is an essential part of helping her learn to become an emotionally independent adult.

7. Pay attention to your daughter's emotional responses

It would be best to find out why your daughter is feeling so angry and stressed by offering her some of your undivided attention. Listen to what she has to say and allow her to express herself without interruptions. This approach will enable you to connect with her while creating a sense of balance between you.

8. Find common ground

Find common interests and things you can do together, such as taking a trip or walking in the park. This can help keep your relationship intact, primarily when stressful problems like school or bullying occur.

9. Be patient

Your daughter will tell you about things in her life, even when it is not the most convenient time to talk about them. For example, your daughter may feel embarrassed and ashamed when afraid of being bullied at school, but she may not be able to say why. Be willing to give her time and space to express herself about anything bothering her. How you deal with the problems you face with your daughter is the key to maintaining a good relationship between the two of you.

Schedule a time to discuss the issues you are facing with your daughter and discuss them at an appropriate time when your daughter feels calm, relaxed, and comfortable. Ask questions about how your daughter feels, what she thinks about everything that is going on, and how you can help her.

Don't get distracted by all the problems when these conflicts arise; instead, try to focus on one conflict at a time. Focus on accepting your daughter for who she is and not pressuring her to change her behavior or actions. which means that you will have to learn to deal with some unacceptable behaviors.

If you can do this, there should be a strong chance that your daughter will begin to have more trust in you because she knows that you love and care about her. Be patient with your daughter as she grows up, for sometimes, the best way to learn about life is through trial and error.

Follow the guidelines above when handling these difficult situations and your relationship with your daughter to stay intact. In addition, your daughter will no longer be afraid to express herself openly and honestly with you. She will also feel secure enough to communicate with you about any problems that she is experiencing. The more your daughter trusts you, the better off she will be being angry at your daughter won't help the situation, it will more likely cause resentment and make your daughter more resistant to change because of how others perceive her negatively.

Try to find time to do something fun and relaxing to help you stay balanced. You will also want to use all the resources available from your family and friends. When your daughter is acting up, it can be easy to lose sight of the positive things she does in her life. An excellent way to bring balance back into your life is by focusing on how she has overcome her difficulties - by doing well at school, making positive changes in her life and relationships with others, or just by being happy and relaxed most of the time.

Chapter 3

Recognizing the Signs of a
Strained Relationship

It's not always easy to tell when a relationship is starting to become strained. Mother-daughter relationships are no exception. Daughters grow up and reach the age where they're starting to become independent yet need their mom's unconditional love, protection, and guidance. Daughters must feel their mother is aware of all facets of their life. While this is a natural part of a budding, healthy relationship, there will be times when both mother and daughter may be feeling frustrated with one another.

So, it is essential to remain empathetic to your daughter and understand her point of view while still maintaining your feelings. When you catch yourself getting frustrated with your daughter or having an attitude, make sure you recognize it, stay connected, and work to address the issue in order to prevent a further disconnect.

Understanding the signs of a strained mother-daughter relationship

The mother-daughter relationship is one of the most important relationships for any woman, it can be a source of strength, support, and love throughout life. However, there can also be times when this relationship becomes strained.

It's important to understand the signs of a strained mother-daughter relationship in order to identify the issues and take steps toward resolving them.so It is crucial to recognize which type of relationship you have with your daughter. Some signs of a strained relationship can include tense conversations, lack of communication, disagreements over values and boundaries and an increase in conflict. Rather than relying on an argument or fight to resolve issues or problems that come up daily, try to focus on problem-solving and working together toward a common goal or solution.

So, what are the common signs of a strained mother-daughter relationship?

Be on the lookout for these red flags to determine if your daughter is fed up with fighting and arguing with you.

If you ask your daughter repeatedly to do something, but she continues to refuse or procrastinate, you may need to evaluate her reaction to your requests. She might feel that it's an overwhelming request that she would rather not comply with at all rather than making an effort, then this may be a sign of a strained relationship.

If you find yourself stepping in to take over every aspect of your daughter's life and are constantly making decisions for her, then it is likely that the relationship has become strained. It's essential to make sure that you respect your daughter's needs and help her grow into an independent adult without becoming overbearing.

The relationship may be strained if your daughter is intentionally difficult, and you feel she's putting you through unnecessary stress. If she thinks you're too strict, you may need to change your approach and tone to suit her needs better.

Sometimes relationships are one-sided, and it's hard for one person to figure out what is causing the tension.

If your daughter is in a phase of her life where she isn't feeling like getting close to anyone and feels as though she's completely independent, it might be difficult for you to feel as though you have a strong relationship with her. just take the time to understand and communicate with her avoiding tension and criticism.

It may seem as if your relationship depends on the simplest tasks, such as completing homework or chores around the house. It's important to communicate what and when needs to be done.

While it is essential to maintain your own space and not be overbearing, you may also need to look at your methods of discipline. Find yourself becoming increasingly frustrated with your daughter's inability or unwillingness to listen or follow through with requests. This could be a sign that her respect for you is diminishing.

A strained mother-daughter relationship is one in which apologies are not made, and unnecessary tension often prevails over a common goal or purpose. By understanding the signs of a strained mother-daughter relationship and what can be done to avoid these problems, you can ensure that your relationship with your daughter remains healthy even after she has grown up.

What are some of the factors that may be causing the strain?

Struggles in relationships are often caused by problems that are deeper than the surface. To truly understand what is causing a strained relationship, it's essential to look at each problem from a deeper level. If you look at the situation from a broader perspective, you will gain insight into why things are happening and the best way to work on them.

If your daughter feels as though she has an equal amount of say in all aspects of her life, then it is unlikely that there will be any strain on the relationship. But if one party feels they have no say in the other's decisions, this can cause frustration and stress.

There are other factors that contribute to a strained mother-daughter relationship such as:

- Different parenting styles.
- Different or unreasonable expectations of each other
- Unrealistic expectations or demand for attention or approval
- Differences in values and beliefs
- Poor or lack of communication
- The use of intensive language and hurtful words.

In some cases, a strained mother-daughter relationship may be caused by something that has happened in the past.

For example, if your daughter has experienced an emotionally traumatic event, she may find it challenging to feel comfortable with how things are at home.

In these situations, it is best to try to work with her and ensure she understands that you love her and want what is best for her.

Steps to fixing a dysfunctional relationship and rebuilding trust

The mother-daughter relationship is a unique and complex bond that is often filled with love but can sometimes experience conflict. When two people with such a close connection experience tension, it can be difficult to overcome and can leave both people feeling hurt or frustrated.

However, it is possible to re-establish a healthier, more positive relationship by addressing the underlying issues, honoring effective communication and problem-solving strategies, and engaging in honest conversations.

The following steps can be helpful when it comes to repairing a strained relationship with your daughter:

1. Apologize

It can be challenging to admit to your daughter that you've been wrong, but it is the first step in repairing any relationship. If you don't feel like apologizing will help, then try taking your daughter out for dinner or something she likes to do. If this still doesn't seem to work, then maybe it is time to find someone else to help you with the situation.

2. Listen

If your daughter is not fully open to forgiving you and working on the relationship, try listening to her and letting her know that she can talk about anything with you.

3. Be patient

If your daughter is struggling with a strained mother-daughter relationship, then it can take time for her to rebuild it. Try not to let her push your buttons and remain patient. If she is angry with you for something that happened in the past, it may be best to focus, listen, and repair.

4. Forgive

You will want to forgive your daughter for her past actions, but it is also important to remember that you have might have been wronged. If you can't find a way to forgive her for what she's done, then you will likely never be able to repair the strained relationship.

5. Make sure that things are always moving forward

Once you have tried to repair the strained mother-daughter relationship, it is essential not to fall back into old habits and routines. You want your daughter's trust back permanently, and this won't happen unless you remain consistent with everything in the relationship.

6. Stay calm

It can be straightforward to become angry when your daughter says or does something wrong, but it can also be beneficial when working on repairing the strained mother-daughter relationship. Just because your daughter makes a mistake doesn't mean there is no hope of repairing the damaged relationship. She may feel like there is nothing she can do to make things right, but being calm and understanding will help her move forward from the situation.

7. Learn from your mistakes

No matter how difficult it may be, it is essential to try and learn from the mistakes that you have made in the past. This can include ensuring you don't do anything that could worsen the strained mother-daughter relationship. If there is something that you did wrong, then try not to let it happen again.

8. Encourage her to trust you

It can be difficult for your daughter to work on repairing the strained mother-daughter relationship when she doesn't feel like she can trust you, but she needs to find a way for herself to believe in you again and believe in herself. If you can stay calm and encouraging, you will be able to help her find a way back to a healthier relationship.

9. Try again

If you cannot work on the mother-daughter relationship by yourself, you may want to enlist the help of another family member or friend. If you find that a close friend can help but still can't get through to your daughter, it's time to look for a professional specializing in relationships.

It will take a lot of hard work and dedication, but the result will be worth it when you have an effective mother-daughter relationship that brings peace to both parties.

Please work with your daughter and try not to let her push your buttons. When it comes to having an excellent mother-daughter relationship, it is essential to remember that you are on the same team and have the same goals, and when it comes to repairing a strained mother-daughter relationship, there are various ways that you can approach the situation with your daughter.

The goal is to fix your relationship with your daughter so you're both happy again. Remember that repairing a strained mother-daughter relationship will take time and patience. It will not happen overnight, but it is possible if you put your mind to it. You have been a good mother to your daughter, and you deserve the same in return.

Chapter 4

Bridging the Gap

The mother-daughter relationship is one of the most powerful and rewarding connections a girl will ever have. for many daughters, their mother is their source of strength, encouragement, and guidance. However, it's not always easy to maintain a harmonious mother-daughter bond, and communication breakdowns can lead to tension and conflicts causing an inevitable gap between them. Perhaps it's inevitable that this gap will form between you and your daughter as you grow up, but you don't have to let it get too wide.

Bridging this gap requires honest dialogue and both parties working together to create and sustain a healthy relationship, with awareness and effort, a mother and daughter can repair a fractured relationship and strengthen the bond between them.

Building a relationship with your daughter is not an easy task. You might have to work at it while they struggle with a rebellious streak, and your patience is exhausted. Nevertheless, when you finally see progress in the relationship and the two of you are on the same page, there's nothing better than a bond that lasts a lifetime.

Building an enduring friendship with your daughter is not about being "best friends." It's about making them feel comfortable enough for both parties to be open about their feelings and ask for help when needed. It's about standing by each other through thick and thin, through good and bad times.

Understanding the social changes in your daughter's life

Social changes are probably the most significant source of stress for you and your daughter. She is changing faster than you can ever imagine, which makes it hard for you to adjust. The mother-daughter relationship has a natural ebb and flow, with communication ebbing when she's grown up. You might feel as if you have to hold on, yet the time is coming when both of you will be ready to let each other go. This can be a painful and lonely time for you, but it's essential to understand that it happens to all mothers and daughters.

The most important thing to remember is that your daughter is changing, which means she wants a new kind of relationship with you now. Let her adjust to the changes and embrace the opportunities that come from independence.

Your relationship will grow stronger as she stands on her own two feet; this is when you can make your mark on her life. You should introduce a new kind of honesty into your relationship; focus on emotional honesty instead of saying the right words.

How does social change in your daughter's life affect your role as a parent and the relationships you have with your daughter?

The role of a mother is to recognize and respond to the social changes in her daughter's life while continuing to guide and support her. as your daughter transitions from childhood to adulthood, she'll naturally begin to take more responsibility for her own life and from her own individual identity.

During this process, it may be difficult for parents to discern the appropriate level of guidance and support to provide their daughter.

Having a consistent, honest dialogue between mother and daughter, and maintaining flexible and open communication, are the essential steps to navigating the changing emotional, social, and psychological needs of a daughter without compromising the loving relationship between mother and daughter. doing so can create an unparalleled bond between you and your daughter that is enriched by mutual respect and understanding. As her mother, you must understand what changes need to be made. Maybe it will be expected of her to start making decisions on her own sooner than planned, and this is when your role as mom needs to shift away from being the all-knowing parent who dictates everything about life for her.

As your daughter is finding her place in society, she will need your support and encouragement. You can encourage her by becoming a trusted friend. She might need to vent her feelings and tell you about the problems she's having, but it should be your role to set the tone for this relationship. Remember that your relationship with your daughter is more than just her mother and daughter.

Regardless of how she feels about you, you are a good friend who will help guide her on her journey through life. Giving your daughter the freedom, she needs, while being open with both of you about what's happening, is the only way to ensure your relationship will endure. Allowing your daughter to grow up and embrace independence, while still having a close mother-daughter bond, is a win-win situation all around.

A strong mother-daughter bond can help to bring them both closer together and give them the support they need when one of them needs it most.

It's good to remember that change is inevitable; all we can do is find ways to make it as comfortable as possible. It's also important not to allow your relationship with your daughter to be altered. there is no need for an ongoing discussion about the changes in her day-to-day life.

How to be an active and involved part of your daughter's life, despite the gap

Being an active and involved mother in your daughter's life, despite the gap created by her transition into adulthood is possible with the right approach.

As your daughter is finding her place in society, she will need your support and encouragement. You can encourage her by showing your sincere interest and involvement in her life by spending quality time together, engaging in meaningful conversations, selecting carefully the topics for discussion, and offering loving guidance and encouragement.

Here are a few ideas to help you bridge the gap between you and your growing up daughter:

1. Communication

Mothers and daughters have a unique challenge in communicating with each other. The language of love is often different from one generation to another. However, talking together about your thoughts, emotions, and dreams will help build a strong foundation for the future.

At an early age, encourage your daughter to express herself freely and openly with you—and don't be afraid of "mother-daughter talk." Talk about everything from feelings, career, and education plans to emotions like anger or sadness. Share your hopes and dreams for your daughter as well.

2. Distraction

Distraction can be a powerful tool to help your daughter deal with her feelings or an experience at school or with friends. You might try to help her forget by watching a movie together, going shopping or out for ice cream, or letting her paint a picture to express herself with words or pictures.

You can also offer her a complete distraction by bundling her up and taking her out for a fun day of shopping or brunch. Make the day count with experiences that mean something to you.

3. Privacy

Even though you know your daughter better than anyone else, you can only know so much about her. She needs to learn to manage her privacy and keep some things to herself.

Don't take this the wrong way – you're a parent, and it's your job to help when your daughter needs it. However, sometimes, she'll have to figure things out independently. Give her some space to live into her little world, that helps her become more confident and creative.

4. Independence

Respect her adulthood and independence along with her decisions and freedom this will help to build trust and open communication with your daughter. Give her that independence and let her know she'll be able to solve most of the issues by herself when she's ready.

5. Spend some time together

Instead of waiting for an event or a special occasion to spend more time with your daughter, make the time right now. Find out what she likes and what she doesn't like to do. Offer to help her plan a party or find a movie that both of you can enjoy so you can spend quality time together.

You might also want to invite your daughter's friends over for dinner so she can spend some time with her friends while you're there.

Time spent together is one of the best ways to rekindle a relationship and show her that you'll be there for her no matter what. It's good for your daughter to know what you like and dislike so she can help plan some activities for you too.

6. Respect

Respect is a two-way street; let your daughter know how much you respect her for being who she is. The bond between mother and daughter will be strengthened, and she'll know you care about what she has to say.

When your daughter sets goals for herself, be supportive by encouraging her to keep at them until she reaches them. If possible, offer help when you can without doing everything for her.

7. Encourage

When it comes to your daughter's appearance, abilities, or feelings, encourage her to express herself by talking about what's going on in her life.

Show your daughter you care about her by hugging her, kissing her, and telling her that you support what she does. Always show your daughter how much you love and care for her by expressing yourself with words of encouragement. Empower your daughter to set goals for herself by helping her achieve them.

If you see that your daughter is interested in something, whether it's a new attribute or a skill she's been practicing, encourage her and give her the tools to try different things.

It would be best to encourage your daughter when you see that she's sad or depressed – it may be because of something going on at school or with friends, so let her know you've noticed the change.

8. Stay Involved

Get involved with your daughter's life, but don't smother her. It's essential to show your daughter that you're interested in what she does and what she likes.

You can show interest without being an overbearing parent – give yourself some slack and let things happen naturally. If you want to strengthen your relationship with your daughter, get involved without making it seem like you're trying too hard.

Stay involved in your daughter's life, by standing firm where morals and values are involved and always choosing to show your unconditional love, and support and don't expect anything from your relationship. Offer help, guidance, and advice without being invasive or intrusive to the point where she no longer feels like sharing.

Being active in your daughter's life is one of the best ways to rekindle a relationship with her and help her grow up as a responsible adult.

Remember to keep an open mind and think about what's best for her; she'll appreciate it when you support her by not being judgmental or giving her too much advice.

If you want to rekindle the mother-daughter bond, communicate regularly with your daughter and make time for her without expecting anything from the relationship.

Don't try to solve every problem or fix everything for your daughter – allow her to grow up, become independent and make mistakes.

Chapter 5

Being a Student of Your Daughter

Being a student is watching and listening to what your daughter has to say about her world, who she is, and how she sees herself. It means that you're giving her feedback on the things that are important to her, asking for support when you need it, and ensuring that she knows all the little details about your life, so she'll be able to reconnect with you later in life.

As a mother, you have a special opportunity to be a student of your daughter's transition into adulthood. by understanding the changes, she is going through, the challenges she faces, and the decisions she must make, you can build a strong and healthy relationship.

Most importantly, it means being an open adult with your daughter. which is the key here because this type of relationship allows both sides to feel safe opening up about anything they want.

Interacting with your daughter is a powerful and intimate relationship that will last for the rest of her life. To have this kind of relationship, you must be open and honest with her.

As a parent, paying attention to what your daughter is trying to say is essential because they tell us things through their behaviors. additionally, make sure to remain respectful of her independence, decisions and choices, that will show her that she is values. By taking the time to be a student of your daughter, you will be able to strengthen your relationship and help her grow into a confident and resilient adult.

Understanding the importance of studying your daughter's natural personality

Being a mother, it is important to take the time to understand your daughter's unique characteristics and personality, through studying her interests, abilities and goals. Furthermore, understanding and what she wants out of life can provide you with valuable insight into how you can best support her during this time of growth. Learning to appreciate the person your daughter is now, as well as spotting and nurturing her potential, is a key part of helping her make successful transitions into adulthood. You can better understand your daughter if you identify her personality type; then, you can begin to study her natural traits and behaviors.

Your daughter naturally has a unique DNA and therefore a unique personality, and like all of us, she will interact with the world very differently depending on her moods and circumstances.

While knowing that you cannot change your daughter's natural personality is essential, it is equally essential to be aware that you can change how you interact with her.

When you study her personality and use all your senses, you are communicating with her at a much deeper level than words. By learning about who she is and what she values, you can create a vision for the relationship you want with her.

The importance of studying your daughter's natural personality includes the following:

1. **Understanding your daughter better and recognizing the truth about her**

You cannot understand your daughter as well as you can through conversation and watching her personality. This can not only be interesting and exciting to you, but it will also be invaluable for a successful relationship in the future.

The more you understand your daughter, the more natural boundaries you create so that there are no misunderstandings or conflicts. You can view life together as you want it to be with her; it'll just come naturally because of how much you feel connected.

2. Understanding how to get your daughter to do what you want her to do

If you do not understand your daughter through her personality, it's harder to ensure that your will is fulfilled.

Have conversations with your daughter about what you are experiencing, sharing the moments and asking her for feedback on important issues.

When you communicate with each other regularly, she will be more apt to cooperate and communicate with you in return. The more you communicate with your daughter, the more likely you will get her to do what you ask her to without an argument.

3. Understanding how to express your love and positive feelings toward your daughter

It's incredibly important for a mother to demonstrate her love for her daughter in tangible ways, by listening to her worries, fears, and questions. Show her that she is values, appreciated by being supportive and provide physical affection as well as verbal praises, never be afraid of showing emotion, it will benefit her in the long run. The more positive influence you have on her life, the more she builds self-confidence and self-love.

4. Understanding of how to show your support and be compassionate toward your daughter

If you are talking about a situation or problem with your daughter and you are the first person willing to listen, it will significantly impact her. She can feel the support she wants, to keep herself stable and secure. The more you allow her to be herself, the less likely she will have problems with trust.

5. Understanding how to create good boundaries for your daughter

Setting reasonable boundaries between yourself and your daughter will make her feel more stable and secure. When she knows that you care about her, it's easier for her to accept the boundaries you have set for her. She will also be more willing to trust your judgment by listening to what she thinks is right or wrong instead of doing whatever she wants just because it's outside your rules.

6. Understanding of how the world works for her

When discussing an issue with your daughter, you can help her understand why certain things happen and how the world works (in a light-hearted way). This way, she will be able to move forward into the future and have more confidence when it comes to seeing different situations that are presented to her.

The more you understand your daughter, the better you can set up a good foundation for future disputes. Your daughter will trust you more and feel safe in the relationship. When she feels safe and secure with you, she is less likely to have problems trusting others or herself.

Lastly, your goal is to facilitate her successful transition into adulthood, by building confidence, respecting her individual differences and strengths, gaining insights into her goals and life plans, appreciating who she is now and nurturing her potential. This way you will build the strong connecting you are looking for.

How to understand and appreciate your daughter's unique characteristics

As a mother, understanding your daughter's personality will help you develop a better relationship with her. Understanding characteristics and seeing the world through her eyes will allow you to take steps to improve your relationship with each other.

If you truly want a healthy and rewarding relationship with your daughter, you must clearly understand how she sees the world around her. Ask questions about the different issues in your lives together and listen to what she has to say about them.

If there is anything you don't understand, ask yourself if it's important enough or just something superficial.

When you try to understand your daughter's personality and how she sees the world around her, you can take steps to be more accepting of her views.

The better you understand your daughter's characteristics, the more likely your relationship with her will have a much better future ahead of it.

How do you understand and appreciate your daughter's unique characteristics?

It's much simpler to appreciate how your daughter sees the world when you get to know her personality.

Because your daughter is honest and upfront with you, you can be more accepting and understanding of how she perceives the world. Understanding that your daughter is different from everyone else will attract others with similar views or views on things.

These people will be able to connect with your daughter because of how similar they all are. You can understand and appreciate your daughter's unique characteristics in the following ways:

1. Show her your appreciation

It's essential to show your appreciation for everything that she does and everything that contributes to the relationship. This will allow her to feel good about herself for being a good person and doing the right thing.

With love and appreciation, she will feel a greater sense of self-esteem and confidence. She will feel confident that you find her special enough so that you can treat her with a lot of grace and respect.

2. Don't try to change her

When your daughter has a vision of whom she would like herself to be in the future and what she dreams about being when she grows up, she might have a good idea of how capable or incapable she is of handling certain situations in life.

It would be best if you do not try to change her into the person you think she should be. If you were to encourage her to be more of the person, she feels she should be, then she might feel unaccepted by the world around her.

3. Don't be quick to judge her

If you are too quick to judge your daughter without hearing her out, then it will only hurt her more in the future. Your daughter will feel more confident that you take time out of your day to listen to what she has to say. This will help her make decisions about her life that make her feel more confident and prouder.

4. Please do your best to understand her

When you try to understand your daughter's personality, it will be easier for her to trust you. Your daughter will feel a lot more understanding toward how you treat her because of what she has gone through with others.

If you are willing to do your best for her to respect herself, then she will do her best in return and be more willing to show what she has within herself.

When you understand what her personality is like, then you won't be surprised by anything coming up in the future.

When you are surprised by her behavior, it can frustrate both of you and make communication difficult. so just take a deep breath and restart! Things will eventually become smooth.

5. Be patient

Being patient with your daughter is key to understanding her unique characteristics, and it starts with your attitude and approach. acknowledge her feeling and be open to her perspective, then take the time to really listen to her, be supportive and encouraging, ask questions, offer ideas, and be patient. Finally, be sure to practice positive reinforcement- a positive approach goes a long way!

She will feel more confident when you are patient with her because she won't have to worry about being judged in the long run. Seeing things from her perspective can help her ease her mind about what could happen if she starts being herself.

6. Observe the way that your daughter acts and talks

Your daughter's actions and talks can show how she sees things more deeply. The more you can communicate with her the more you will be able to understand who she is as a person. When you're having conversations, please pay attention to the topic of conversation and how she moves through it.

Your daughter will be more at ease when she is talking about things that she is passionate about or cares about deeply. She will give off signals when she isn't interested in talking about something because of how uncomfortable she feels in those situations.

7. How your daughter responds to things that happen in the world

When you are having a conversation with your daughter, it's essential for you not to judge her responses and actions. Please pay attention to how she behaves around others and how she acts when something is happening in the world. She will act out of character when she is around someone who makes her uncomfortable.

Your acceptance and appreciation of their unique personality can be seen in how they act around people or when something happens in their lives.

When they are around people, they don't like, or whom they don't like, they will be more open and comfortable in the situation. They will feel safer around these people because of how much they trust their own opinions.

Chapter 6

What Daughters Need from
Their Mothers?

$\mathcal{A}$s a mom, you need to learn more about your daughter so she can talk to you like an adult. It doesn't matter how old your daughter is; most importantly, they learn independence and autonomy at their own pace. As a mother, you might want to know everything about your daughter and if she has a proper diet, what her current friends like, how many hours she spends on social media, etc. It's normal to want to be aware of all the essential things in your child's life. However, it could be the wrong approach when you try to show her that you know everything. It will only make her feel restless with your nagging and controlling behavior.

As a mother, you need to trust your daughter and let her grow at her own pace. One of the most important things you can give your daughter is your time. Make sure she knows she can talk to you when needed. Make her feel special by spending quality time together, providing emotional support and guidance, and modeling positive behavior.

You need to know that you have unique insights and knowledge into your daughter's needs, so make sure to encourage honest communication and strive to understand her feeling, thoughts, and beliefs. ultimately, daughters need to know that they are respected and safe while they explore and grow. But it doesn't mean that it must be done in the same pattern daily. You shouldn't force spending time with her just because you think she needs it; otherwise, she will feel suffocated by too much attention and will act out even more.

Understanding the unrevealed needs and desires of daughters

As your daughter grows up, you must be willing to discover her needs and desires. You can't expect her to open up when you push her or not listen. Some daughters have a strong bond with their mothers, but some don't want to talk about what is happening in their life. It may seem strange for a mother, but she knows what she wants. By ignoring the statements that "she doesn't want to share with me" or "there isn't any chance for us to talk about anything personal," you are missing one of the greatest opportunities to get closer as a family and create an everlasting bond with each other.

It would be best if you put your need-to-know things aside. You have to be open-minded and patient to understand if your daughter has serious problems, she can't share them with you.

It is not a sign of weakness and doesn't mean she does not trust you! If she is struggling with something, the last thing she wants to do is discuss it.

It takes a lot of courage for a woman to open up about her feelings, especially when personal discussing issues requires vulnerability. Daughters can have a difficult time telling you what they need from you. Due to different reasons, daughters might not be able to express their feelings openly.

You need to understand that your daughter has her problems and struggles. Try asking her about what she is going through and what she likes and dislikes. Be ready to listen and give your advice with love and empathy.

If she needs you to do something specific or go to a place together, do respect her wishes and give her your time. Sometimes it's not about what you want but what she wants. Let her have the space to express her feelings without your interference.

How do you understand the unrevealed needs and desires of daughters:

1. Empathy is an essential quality to have.

Your daughter wants your time and attention. Listen to her and try to understand her doubts or fears.

2. Give her space.

If your daughter wants to go out alone with her friends and you are worried about it, why is it that serious for you? Think of the ways you can deal with that situation calmly and maturely. Don't react irrationally because it might cause more damage to you.

3. Be patient with your daughter

When she is sad or angry at you even if you don't understand why she feels that way. Hug her; maybe she needs to be held when feeling down. Show her your care and love by doing something nice for her, like cooking a meal she likes or making it in her favorite color.

4. Try to find time for activities you both enjoy.

This is a perfect way to bond. It doesn't matter what you do together if both of you are happy and having fun.

5. Be honest with your daughter

Talk to her about how lucky she is to have a mom who loves her unconditionally and will make everything possible to make her happy.

6. Be careful when asking questions

Do so while trying to understand your daughter's needs and desires but don't ask too many questions at once because it might be too much for her to tolerate at one time, and she will shut down completely.

7. Encourage her to be herself

Don't try to change her by making her think that she can't do something quickly or there are a few things she shouldn't do. If she is having a tough time doing something, let her know it will be okay and show her the way.

8. Let your daughter know

Tell her that you are always around so that whenever she feels like talking, she can call you up and tell you everything about what happened in school or at home.

9. Be unpredictable with your daughter

Let her see how indifferent you are to specific subjects, and make sure not to go overboard with her.

10. Try to set specific rules

This is so your daughter knows the limits she can't cross. You should know what is okay and what is not okay for a kid, but don't make her feel like you are judging her because you have specific rules for her to follow.

You need to be aware that feelings and emotions can be tricky things to talk about, especially if you are very close with your daughter. However, it would be best to learn how to talk about it. The harder you try, the easier it will become for you two.

It's not easy to understand the unrevealed needs and desires of daughters it can be helpful to have a listening ear and to foster an open dialogue with them. The best way to communicate is to consider asking thoughtful questions and being present and in tune with them.

You should not push your daughter into expressing anything, because she has to be ready for any dialogue between the two of you to start. There are various reasons daughters don't want to talk to their mothers. It doesn't make them weak; it makes them intelligent enough to figure out that they don't need you. The best thing you can do is be okay with this and cherish the time you have spent together. Make sure she knows how much you care for her and that the time will come for her to do the same thing with her future child with the same love and care.

How to fulfill those needs and create a deeper bond with your daughter

Give your daughter the time she needs when she's ready to talk. Don't force it; if you do, she will not want to tell you anything because of the uncomfortable feeling it creates. You should always respect your daughter's wishes and let her be in control of her life.

1. Be consistent.

Treating her like a kid or an adult is unnecessary here because what she needs from you is the same as any other girl would need from their mother. Please ensure you always keep her expectations in mind by always being there for her whenever she needs anything and telling her the importance of the relationship you two have built together. Sometimes we don't realize how much our children understand us until it is too late, so make sure that she knows how important this bond is to you.

2. Please don't do anything that will hurt her.

It is important to make decisions that are in her best interest and protect her safety and well-being. it's also important to consider her feelings and take them into account when making decisions.

3. Set clear boundaries between mother and daughter.

It's essential to have rules in the relationship and not cross them without discussing them first. You need to know how many restrictions you can set on her without becoming unbearable. Make sure you know what's appropriate for a kid and what's not. That way, you won't have any bad consequences with your daughter because she knows where to draw the lines, and if she crosses them, there will always be a consequence that she must face.

4. Help her build her self-esteem by letting her know how much you appreciate everything she does for you.

Don't belittle what she does because that doesn't help her; it will force her to make herself feel even worse about it and make you feel bad too.

5. Be a good example.

being a good example for your daughter starts with being an authentic example of the qualities you wish for her to have. This means demonstrating respect, selflessness, kindness, empathy, thoughtfulness, courage, and honesty.

Set a good example for her by being responsible, reliable, and organized. Take time to talk and listen to her carefully, read and learn together, create a safe and secure environment, be honest in all situations, and most importantly, show unconditional love and acceptance. What she sees is what she will want in life, so make sure that you are making her see that you are a great person to be around, that you have deep values and morals.

When you show your daughter how much respect you have for yourself, you will start making a great example of how a person should treat others in many ways.

6. Don't take small things too seriously

Try to see the humor in everything. This will make everything less stressful for her and make sure that no matter what happens in life, she has someone to have fun with when she is not feeling too great about herself.

Sometimes, she will refuse to talk to you about something because she needs some time to be alone. It doesn't mean that she doesn't like you or is mad at you; it just means that sometimes, we don't want to talk to anyone. Don't try to keep her talking because sometimes, it can be confusing and overwhelming. Just let her know that you love her and always be there for her whenever she is ready to open up and talk.

7. Don't be afraid to ask her what she needs from you when feeling down about something.

Please get to know her feelings and respond accordingly because sometimes, a girl must figure things out for herself.

8. Stay curious about your daughter's life.

Ask her questions about it and show that you want the best for the person you raise. This will make her feel like she has someone who cares about her, which is what she needs from you.

As you can see, you should take the time to protect your relationship with your daughter because she is your little girl and that means she needs you. She needs to know what a great mother you are, how much you love her, and how important it is for her to live a happy life.

Suppose you can take the time to set up and maintain a great relationship with your daughter. In that case, she will not complain, and she will always feel like there is someone who cares about her, so make sure that you don't let any negativity come in the way of your relationship. If you take these tips and use them as a guide for yourself, you will be able to form a great relationship with your daughter, which leads to lifetime happiness.

Chapter 7

It's Never Too Late to Get
Back on Track

It's never too late to get back on track in the mother-daughter relationship matter the age gap, communication is the key to building a strong and lasting bond between a mother and daughter.

Keeping the lines of communication open can help both individuals. Appreciate each other's unique perspectives and learn from each other. Taking the time to listen and be present for each other can create a deep foundation for honest and meaningful conversations.

These wholesome conversations, based on mutual trust and respect, can help reduce misunderstandings and prevent miscommunication. Better still, the mother-daughter relationship can create a gateway for beautiful experiences and cherished moments.

Building a healthy relationship with your daughter can begin now, even before puberty starts. It's never too late to start because you can be hands-on with your daughter in her teenage years. You can also ease into the conversation by talking casually and acting like a friend.

You want her to know that this is the relationship you want to that will help her navigate life as she grows. She will have someone to talk to, who listens and cares about her. This is the foundation of your daughter's best friend-you!

Recognizing that it's never too late to mend a relationship with your daughter

It's never too late to get back on track with your daughter. As a mother, you want what's best for her and she deserves the best. You had the opportunity to shape her life while she grew in your womb and now you can continue to mold her into the woman she will become outside of it. In order to make your bond everlasting, it's necessary that you show her how much you care. You want to be the woman she looks up to because you are also her role model. She needs you in her life for more than just a couple of years because her role model will help her become herself and make better choices in life. Make sure you are a strong presence in her life.

It is extremely difficult to walk away from her when you're busy, but it's incredibly important that she understands that you'll always be there for her. Show your daughter how much she means to you by making time to connect with her on a regular basis.

You can do this by taking her to the movies, or on a play date and just spending some time together. You want to make it clear that there is no one else she can count on as much as she does with you. Your number one job as a mom is to keep her safe.

It's never too late to renew and strengthen the mother-daughter relationship. respect and understanding lay the foundation for positive interactions between mother and daughter. Start by listening to each other's perspectives and points of view without judgment. Embrace each other's mistakes and learn from the disappointments instead of blaming and shaming.

Validate each other's feelings and be gentle and patient in words used and actions are taken. Nothing is more precious than being able to cherish each other's company after the renewal and mending of the relationship.

It's never too late to start again because together is always better!

Preserve your relationship with your daughter because that will help you make the right choices in life. You will gain a daughter for life if you give her the positive attention she deserves. Your bond as mother and daughter is unique; make it last forever by being there for her every step of the way. Do your best to make her smile every day because life gets so busy and our kids are bogged down with busy work, we can sometimes forget just how special each one of them is.

The relationship you build with your daughter is truly special because it's so personal and even though it's not life-threatening, sometimes it may feel like it is. You want to make sure you have a healthy bond so that you can spend your whole lives together as mother and daughter.

Her life is constantly changing and it's important she knows how to deal with it. The way to do this is by being open about her feelings, but also letting her know that you will always be there for her no matter what. She needs your support because she's trying to figure out this whole world on her own and running into the wrong people is inevitable.

Being an amazing mother is not an easy job but it's the most rewarding job if done correctly. You will gain the love and respect of many people in your life, but most importantly your child. You need to make sure you take care of yourself so that you can make the most out of yourself as a mother. Sometimes our kids are all we have in this world, and we must protect what's ours because it's the only way they will know how much we truly love them.

You must show your daughter that you really want to be an amazing parent because if you do this, she'll teach herself that it's possible to be an amazing person. Your relationship with her will positively impact her relationships with everyone she comes into contact with and as she grows, so will yours.

Steps to take to become your daughter's best friend, even if you've STRAYED

Every mother and daughter have their ups and downs. Sometimes, it can feel like the two of you are worlds apart from each other and it may be difficult to connect. However, this doesn't mean that your relationship with your daughter is doomed.

The truth is that you will always be her mother, but it doesn't mean that you can't also be friends with her. In fact, these two roles should complement each other because if your daughter sees how much you love her, she will trust you even more.

Here are steps to take to become your daughter's best friend:

1. Look at what made you become distant.

Try to pinpoint the reason why you and your daughter have not been getting along well lately. It could be a one-time event, or it could be something that has built up over time. Either way, you need to find out what caused this rift in your relationship. If you are not sure what made her act this way towards you, ask her so that she can open up to you and tell you how it is.

2. Apologize for whatever made the rift in your relationship happen.

You have to apologize to your daughter because she is not a bad person. She is your child, and you love her no matter what. Whenever you find out that you have hurt her, you need to apologize and then make sure it doesn't happen again. This can show her that you are truly sorry and that you genuinely care about her.

3. Learn from your mistakes.

Try to learn from your mistakes and then do what is necessary to ensure that things don't happen again. Sometimes, it's best to leave a situation between the two of you and never return to it because it can cause problems if left alone, especially when the rift is still existing between the two of you right now. You need to make sure there will be no more negatives in your relationship with your daughter or any other person in your life because these people matter too much for this not to happen.

4. Reinforce that the past is in the past.

Tell your daughter that whatever happened in the past should stay there and never resurface again. Let her know that this is all water under the bridge, and she should not hold it over your head because she knows you are a good person who loves her with all your heart.

5. Spend more time together and do things you both enjoy doing.

Now, you have a chance to get to know each other even more than before because of this opportunity to spend time together doing things you both enjoy. This will help strengthen the bond between mother and daughter so that you don't run into problems anymore like these in the future.

6. Talk to your daughter's friends and other family members.

Another way to build a strong relationship with your daughter is to talk to the people she trusts the most such as her friends, teachers, and other family members. Let them know how much you love her and ask them what they think you can do to help strengthen the bond between you two. You want to keep your daughter's trust because keeping it intact is a sign of strength for both of you.

7. Do not try too hard or get angry if she does not like what you have planned for the two of you together.

Sometimes, she will interpret your gestures as being forced or fake even if that is not true in any way at all. This is because she feels that you are trying too hard to show that you want to get closer to her. Instead, try doing things that the two of you both enjoy but don't force your daughter into it. Let her choose what she wants to do and keep it exchange as simple as possible.

8. Be there for your daughter whenever you can.

Try not to miss out on important occasions in your daughter's life such as birthdays, recitals, and graduations because these are all times when you will have a chance to show her how much you care about the person she has grown up into today. You can reinforce this by encouraging her so that she knows there is nothing she can't accomplish if she puts her mind towards it.

9. Don't be too controlling or overprotective

Allow the daughter to grow by giving her enough space to make her own decision. encourage open and honest communication from both sides. Accept her mistakes and learn from them instead of criticizing her. Focus on her strengths and help her to develop those skills. exchange opinions without judgment and seek mutual understanding instead of always expecting agreements.

10. Stay open-minded and listen to the things your daughter has to say.

This is important because it will help her communicate with you which will build the bond between you two even more. You want to be open-minded so that you can recognize when there are problems that need resolving. It also means that you won't react harshly whenever she does something wrong because she'll feel free and confident enough to share whatever it is that bothers her with you.

Building a strong relationship with your daughter depends on how you should handle several different aspects. You need to make sure that the mistakes you made in the past are not repeated, so try to talk to your daughter and make sure she is not feeling uncomfortable around you so you can have a good time whenever you're together.

It's never too late to improve a relationship between your daughter and you. The earlier you start improving it, the better it will be for the both of you in the future. You need to make sure that your child is not used to being treated badly and forced into doing things she doesn't want to. Instead, make her feel welcomed by making her feel like everything she does is important and valued by you because without those values, she will become bored with life so quickly.

Chapter 8

The Impact of a Mother's Emotional History

There's a very powerful dynamic at play when it comes to mother-daughter relationships. Mothers tend to be the first women a daughter knows and relies on as an emotional support system. This can lead to some of the strongest possibilities for ensuring that your daughter grows up with healthy self-esteem, and endeavors in life, and entwines her identity with your own. A mother's emotional past can also have the potential to impact how she bonds with her daughter, especially if you are coming from a place of fear and low self-esteem.

This bond is so strong that often it can continue to affect the dynamic of your relationship even as your daughter goes through adolescence, leaving many mothers at a loss over how to handle these changes. Feeling the need to stay connected with her daughter but unsure of how to proceed, can lead a mother into making some detrimental choices.

Understanding the impact of a mother's emotional history on her daughter

Although we can't control the original emotional pain in our lives, it is within our power to learn from and heal from these wounds. The things that happen to us and the lessons we learn are vitally important in the formation of an authentic self. They help shape how we see ourselves, how we relate to others, and what boundaries we establish in relationships. If you want your daughter to end up with healthy self-esteem and discover her full potential as a woman, you must be able to work through your emotional traumas as a mother.

One of the main emotional issues a mother may be struggling with is how to relate to her own mother.

This can leave her feeling conflicted because she is torn between wanting to be a good and loving mother and not knowing how to fully understand or forgive the emotional issues that made up her upbringing.

Another common family dynamic is one in which there was little warmth, support, or love and now a daughter feels she must offer this for things to work out between them.

This can leave a daughter feeling like she must be the perfect mother to make up for what is lacking in her core relationship with her mom.

How these dynamics manifest themselves between a mother and daughter varies widely, but they do need to be addressed if you want your daughter to grow and thrive as a woman. As a parent, you want to protect your daughter from the pain of past trauma and whatever issues could hinder her from developing a healthy sense of self. You want to give her the tools needed for resilience and the opportunity for growth, but when she was little, you may have made those very same mistakes yourself.

A mother's emotional history has the following effect on her daughter:

1. Empathy:

It's hard to develop empathy if you are coming from a place of anger and resentment toward yourself or others. As a mother, you have a huge impact on your daughter's ability to develop compassion and empathy for herself, others, and the world around her. If you are unable to find peace within yourself and commit to healing, your daughter can end up with low self-esteem.

2. Self-worth:

If you don't believe that she is worthy of love or respect from others, then she will lack healthy self-worth as well. This can manifest in her relationships with others as well as within her body image by being jealous of other girls who have more enjoyable or fulfilling lives than herself.

3. Strong sense of self:

The most important aspect of this is that the daughter feels a strong sense of worth about herself as a result of being able to develop and honor her own beliefs and values even in the face of peer pressure or other external pressures from family or friends.

4. Boundaries:

A girl with healthy self-esteem can set boundaries intended to protect herself from being taken advantage of by others or feeling like she always needs to put everyone else's needs ahead of her own. Healthy boundaries come from knowing her values and beliefs and deciding what she will or won't do to honor herself and maintain a strong sense of self-worth.

5. Self-care:

Healthy self-esteem and a strong sense of self are directly related to the ability to care for yourself. Self-care is a vital part of this. If a mother is not able to care for herself through healthy practices like eating well and exercising, this can affect how she approaches her daughter. She may feel she doesn't have the time or energy to take care of herself and become over-protective or narcissistically distanced from her child as a result.

6. Trust:

The lack of trust that comes from being emotionally unavailable can lead to mistrust of others in general and your daughter's inner voice about what is real and what is not. If a mother does not trust herself and her instincts, then she will always be on the lookout for deception where there isn't any and will never be able to choose her actions wisely because of this distrust.

What we learn about how to relate to others and our feelings, in general, is learned from our parents. So, when a daughter grows up in an environment where she doesn't feel loved or validated for the things she's feeling, it can make her hesitant to express those same feelings, even when it might be healthy for her. For example, if your mother was very affectionate with you when you were young but later became very detached because she was stressed out, this could lead your daughter to doubt the value of her own needs and emotions. She may start avoiding expressing how she is feeling so that she won't get into trouble or be rejected or abandoned by her mother.

If a daughter grows up witnessing her mother expressing herself in an angry or abusive manner, this can lead her to believe that it's fine to express herself in these ways too.

Just because your mother got angry when you were growing up doesn't mean it's acceptable for you to get angry with your child and should be avoided at all costs. One of the most destructive things that a mother can do to her daughter is withholding love, affection, or even basic care because she is too busy or uninterested.

You may not have realized that you did this as a child, but if it's been going on for years, you are either not aware of what it is doing to your daughter, or you don't care.

If your mother was busy with work during much of your childhood and barely had time to acknowledge how she was neglecting you and not caring for you properly as a child, this can create feelings inside the daughter about being unlovable and undesirable for other reasons beyond just being excessively available.

Steps to recover from emotional absence and prevent it from impacting your daughter's life

Recovery is an important part of the healing process for a daughter who has been emotionally absent from her mother. This healing often leads to a deeper sense of peace as well as respect for yourself and other women. You will also find that you are more respectful of others and have greater compassion toward their feelings and beliefs, including your mom.

You need to acknowledge that you have these feelings about yourself because someone else was unable to care for them properly in the past. As you are working on your recovery, this is where you can give your daughter the same opportunity.

If you have been emotionally absent from her, then she may have similar feelings about her mother. You can be a resource for her as she works through these feelings and learn all the skills, she needs to accept herself, honor herself, and healthily express herself as well.

The steps to recover from emotional absence and prevent it from impacting your daughter's life include:

Step 1: Accept this is how you feel.

The first step is to acknowledge that you do have feelings about yourself. When you can own these feelings as part of your healing, you will then be able to accept them and relate to them as a normal part of life.

You won't feel ashamed for having these feelings or for wanting these things. You will learn how to not only express yourself but honor yourself and in turn, be more available to your daughter.

Step 2: Honor your feelings by letting them go.

Once you have accepted that this is how you feel and why then you are ready to let these feelings go. Feelings are the only beliefs that you have created to help you navigate life. They are not facts, and they are not fixed or true forever.

Feelings can be changed and shifted into different ways of being or they can simply change. When you let go of these feelings, it will relieve some of the pressure and pain that may have been driving them for years. You will also realize that you now can make other choices in your life.

By letting go of these feelings, you strengthen your resilience and be able to bounce back from hardships and challenges better. You will no longer be ruled by your past and can move toward a brighter future for yourself and your daughter.

Step 3: Look for things in your life that feed the feelings and let them go.

The third step is to identify what things are triggering the feelings inside you. This could be certain things that your mother did or said or some other stimulus from the past.

When you have identified what is bothering you, it's important to accept that they are real and that they exist, but they can also be changed.

If you can allow these things to bother you without taking them personally, then it will become easier to choose how to react because of this acceptance. It may take time for you to adjust your reactions or responses to these triggers, but with practice, it will become easier and more comfortable for you.

Step 4: Accept that there are other ways of being.

The fourth step is to learn to enjoy the way you feel when you are with your daughter instead of feeling the intense emotions that were driving them in the past.

Your positive feelings will begin to overflow, and it will become easier and more comfortable for you to be with others in a calm, easy, and loving manner.

Once this step is completed, it's time for your daughter to see how she can develop this skill as well. Once she sees that you can make these positive feelings a reality, then she will learn how to do it as well.

Step 5: Let your daughter know how you feel and how you want her to treat you.

As part of the healing process, your daughter needs to understand how you feel and how she can be there for you as well. It's also important that she understands that these are just feelings and not who she is as an individual or how her life will be on a long-term basis.

It would also help if you told your daughter what things trigger these feelings so that when they happen, she can be prepared and know what to do. This will help your daughter to understand why you are acting a certain way and not always being nice to her.

Step 6: Allow the healing process to take place.

The last step is just like letting all these things go, you need to be willing for this process to take place.

When you step into the space of non-judgment, there is no rush, no judgment happening, and no fight for control. When you allow this healing to take place, you will begin to see the different shades of gray and move from denial to acceptance.

You will no longer be driven by your old beliefs about yourself, but instead, have a new set of beliefs about yourself and your needs and desires. This new way of being can help you be gentler and loving with others because you won't be ruled by negative feelings any longer.

With this process in place, it's time for your daughter to connect with her own emotions and learn how to work through the issues that are bothering her as well.

If she sees and hears how you are working through these old issues, then she will feel safer with you and more comfortable with the idea of sharing her thoughts and feelings with you.

If you allow her to experience the same positive feelings that you are beginning to experience, then she will feel like it's okay for her to be herself as well. When you let go of these feelings with your daughter, you begin to develop a new relationship that is based on respect, love, and trust. This will help her to grow into an independent and positive young woman who can make these same positive feelings a reality in her life. So not only are you helping yourself but your daughter as well.

Chapter 9

Qualities of an Exceptional Mother

A mother must be prepared for all the many changes that come with a child's growth, but it's never too late to build a lasting bond. Moms who want to be best friends and lifelong companions with their daughters need to know what qualities they should seek—and nurture.

An exceptional mother is someone who loves and nurtures her children with kindness and compassion. She is supportive and understanding but also encourages her children to be independent and make their own choices.

She can have difficult, but necessary conversations about topics that can sometimes make kids feel uncomfortable. She sets boundaries and gives clear guidance, but also teaches her children how to be flexible and think critically.

She is there in times of success and difficulty and gives her children the gift of self-confidence and self-worth. An exceptional mother is a great friend, mentor, and protector to her children.

Daughters need more than just a steady supply of motherly love; they especially need the time and attention of their mothers. Mother-daughter time is precious, yet most women find that it is one of the first things they give up when work or family life becomes too hectic. Being there for her daughter is a crucial way for a mom to show the unconditional love she has for her child, it's not just about being physically present.

Identifying the qualities that make a mother exceptional in her daughter's eyes

The first step to being your daughter's best friend is learning and identifying the qualities that make a mother exceptional in her daughter's eyes. Many mothers are afraid they won't be able to meet their daughter's high expectations. They're afraid their imperfections will scare their daughters away, so they bury their insecurities and try to put themselves down instead.

But nothing could be further from the truth. The beauty of this bond is that it's based on respect, honesty, and equality. No matter what has gone on between you in the past, you still have a chance for a very special relationship now – one that's built on mutual respect and self-awareness.

Qualities that make a mother exceptional in her daughter's eyes:

1. An expert listener.

Paradoxically, it's often the most intense moments that require the most listening – when kids are upset and are venting their heartache, explaining why something happened to them, or exhibiting behavior that seems completely out of control.

Mothers who understand how to be good listeners can use that skill to get inside a daughter's mind – not just her emotions – and help her figure out why she's behaving in certain ways.

If you need examples of ways, you've hurt your daughter, tell her about it explicitly and ask for your daughter's forgiveness.

2. A good mediator.

Being a mediator requires you to be able to step back and take a clear-sighted look at the situation. A mother who can do this is accepted by her daughter as an objective and wise counselor.

In this way, she can help her daughter sort out emotional differences with others in the family, among friends, and even on the playground.

Use your mediating skills in situations that don't involve your daughter; it will prove your worth as a trusted, reliable person she can count on – not just when things go wrong with friends or schoolmates, but also when her best friend is mad at her, or their group of girlfriends gets into a fight.

3. An honest and courageous person.

Honesty has a very different meaning to girls. The more secure your relationship is, the more likely she'll be to share difficult things about herself that might upset you or a parent in another part of the family.

But she'll also trust you with her innermost thoughts and feelings, which is what she needs from her grown-up best friend.

4. A strong believer in her daughter's power.

Girls are vulnerable to many societal beliefs about who they are and what they're capable of — that's why mothers need to be role models for their daughters when it comes to valuing personal power.

Help your daughter recognize that she has a right to self-love and confidence and teach her how to access the knowledge that she's capable of handling any situation that arises with grace and self-reliance.

5. A parental guide with a sense of humor.

When confronting different challenges with your daughter — big or small — she needs to know that you have her back and will be there to support her no matter what. In addition to the emotional support you offer, your sense of humor is also key.

Take a lighthearted approach when dealing with problems, so that she doesn't feel overwhelmed and so that she knows you understand that it's hard for a teenager (or anyone) to deal with things like peer pressure or school stressors on their own.

6. A fierce protector.

Being a mother to a daughter means stepping into the role of protector. A good example of this is when your little girl tells you that one of her teachers called her "a brat."

You can help resolve the situation by going directly to her teachers and principal to report the incident and by getting involved in your school and community as an advocate for other girls who may have been humiliated in similar ways.

7. A model of personal growth and self-awareness.

As your daughter grows older, she'll often want you to do something for her that older siblings can help her with – such as picking up a new outfit or bringing in the laundry.

Allow it and reward her for it, but also be a good role model by making time to reflect on her growth and having conversations with her about the ways you feel she's growing up quickly.

By encouraging your daughter to ask you to stay home on school nights, or by setting aside time to go online together and connect with other teens, you can demonstrate your willingness to support her academic growth and development.

8. A compassionate person.

As her best friend, you are a source of support in many situations: You can help her examine where she went wrong or help extricate her from a bad situation with friends or at school.

Help her find solutions to problems and be a sounding board for her concerns. Remember: she's still your baby, and you'll always be there for her – but she has the right to be treated like an adult so that she can take care of herself.

Because you are her mother and closest friend, you have the greatest influence on her personal development. A good mother is willing to place the needs of her daughter first in all situations, and all areas of her life.

Your daughter needs you to be wise, to be a good listener, and the person who acts as the voice of reason. She needs you to be there for her in difficult times, but she also has to learn how to deal with them on her own.

If you are a good mother, your daughter will not have to go it alone as she grows– but instead will have the strength and wisdom of experience, which she'll draw upon as she tackles whatever life throws at her.

How to implement those qualities and become your daughter's best friend

Implementing these qualities in your life is the best way to show your daughter how a woman makes a difference in the world, and why she should be empowered by that.

How do you get started?

Be open about girlhood.

Take an interest in your daughter's school, her friends, and her social scene.

Find books that help you understand what it's like to be a girl today and let her know you read them – they will become important talking points on issues that come up in everyday life.

As you gain insights into how girls are growing up, you'll strengthen the trust between you and your daughter and develop a relationship based on mutual respect and shared learning. Empower your daughter to speak up for herself.

Let your daughter know that she is worthy of respect and deserves to be treated with dignity. It's important to let her know that no matter what happens, you are there for her and believe in her. Tell her you will always be on her side and that you'll protect and fight for her if necessary.

Model self-awareness.

When you're having problems, let your daughter know what they are and how you're dealing with them. If you're struggling with a decision, talk to her about it and invite her to be your sounding board.

The more comfortable you are talking about your own experiences and emotions, the easier it will be for her to approach you with hers.

If she sees that what she's going through is part of life for everyone else, she'll be less likely to think of it as abnormal or shameful, which is especially important during her teen years when peer pressure can have a strong influence on how she thinks and feels about herself.

Practice open dialogue – every day.

Being honest and open with your daughter will allow her to trust you with her life.

She needs to know that she can come to you with her problems and ask for advice, but also that she can talk openly about anything that she's feeling, even if it's scary or embarrassing.

Because your relationship is based on shared understanding, talking openly is the best way to build trust between the two of you.

Be there for her.

Be present in her life as much as you can and help her to learn how to organize her time so that she can do things on her own. Let your daughter know that it's okay to ask you for help when she needs it but be willing to let go of control once she can do something on her own.

Teach her how to make decisions by asking er what decisions she's made in the past and how they went.

Network with other moms.

Connecting with other young women in your area will provide you with a valuable opportunity for friendship and support.

Take an interest in what your daughter's friends are doing and vice versa, acknowledging her accomplishments and encouraging her in her endeavors.

By sharing common interests and making time to get together for dinner or coffee, you can build a strong bond with the girls around you.

Involve your daughter in your life – it's good practice.

Having her involved in chores around the house helps build responsibility and gives her a sense of accomplishment, which are very important traits to develop at this age. Let her be a part of all family traditions and holidays – she'll feel important and involved, and that's very important to your daughter.

If you're still unsure of how to be your daughter's best friend, or if you think that you could use a bit more support and guidance, try incorporating these ideas into your life:

Give your daughter your full attention.

Be sure to go through all the stages of listening to her talk, such as being silent while she's speaking, responding with feedback, summarizing what she has said, and asking questions. If you find it hard to follow this sequence, try making up a list of questions that you can ask her as she talks until, she finishes.

Keep your promises.

You'll lose your daughter's trust if you make a promise and don't follow through. Send a clear message that she is loved, special, and important. If your daughter feels special in your eyes, she will not feel the need to seek approval outside of the home.

Let her know that you're proud of what she's accomplished and how far she's come. Let her know that you believe in her intelligence, creativity, and ability to handle whatever tasks are at hand in life.

Learn about what is going on in her life so that you can be an effective parent. Be there for her as she explores new interests, but also make time to learn about what she's doing and who her friends are.

Be a good role model of healthy relationships with family and friends. Try to get to know her friends on a personal level, but also ensure that she sees you interacting with people positively, without judgment.

Ask your daughter if there is anything you can do to help her – whether it's giving her encouragement or giving her input into something that you're working on at home as a family.

Be aware of the changes in your daughter as she grows up. Help guide her through them so that she doesn't feel overwhelmed or lost in the world. Be a source of comfort when she's feeling insecure or anxious.

Remember that your daughter will reach out to you if she needs you, and make sure that you're always there when she does. Don't be afraid to work on your relationship with your daughter as well as on yourself.

If you two are having a bad day, don't hesitate to give each other some space – but don't be afraid to reconnect later.

Remember that life is an ongoing process, and things won't always come easy for either of you. Stay calm and remember that it's important to have the patience and determination necessary to improve the quality of your relationship with your daughter for years to come.

Chapter 10

A Lifetime Commitment to a
Mother-Daughter Relationship

No matter what stage your daughter is in life, it is always important to build a healthy relationship and find ways to connect with her. When your daughter is an infant, you can bond by sharing in the joy of feeding her and holding her close to you. When she enters the toddler years, make sure she knows that you are interested in what she has to say. As she grows, continue to connect with her by taking time to talk and to do fun things together. At these different stages in her life, you will be her mentor and friend.

Daughters need a mother who is available to listen and who is constantly teaching them about life. To build a solid relationship with her, you can take time each day to be with her and make sure she knows that you are interested in her thoughts and her world.

The best way to create an everlasting bond for a lifetime is to make it a lifetime commitment to a mother-daughter relationship. She will love you for your honesty and for being considerate of her feelings. By taking the time to create a forever bond, you will be helping her build confidence in herself as she grows into an independent young woman.

It is important to spend special time with your daughter every day or even just once or twice a week. Time spent together can be anything! Gardening, cooking together, reading stories, or playing games are great activities to share with your daughter on a regular basis. Just remember that spending quality time daily with her will help create an everlasting bond between the two of you and will result in building trust and respect between each other.

Understanding the importance of an unconditional commitment to a mother-daughter relationship.

The relationship you have with your daughter will be one of the most special relationships you will ever have. It is important that the two of you work to keep the mother-daughter bond strong and healthy. As she grows into a confident young woman, she will need you more than ever. You should never judge her but instead, help her find a way to solve any problems that may arise in her life. Your unconditional commitment to this relationship will help build self-esteem in her and it may even lead her down a path of success as she blossoms into adulthood.

The importance of an unconditional commitment to a mother-daughter relationship is as follows:

1. Building self-esteem.

By making the commitment to an unconditional relationship with your daughter, she will feel that you are there for her and will feel very proud of herself.

You can show that you have confidence in her by sharing her successes and failures and by being there to help her with whatever she may need.

This relationship is a constant source of encouragement for your daughter, who can always come to you when things are going wrong, or she needs guidance.

2. Building trust.

By making an unconditional commitment to a mother-daughter relationship, you will be building trust and respect between both of you. She will know that no matter what happens in her life she can always count on you for support and guidance.

This is an important lesson to teach your daughter. Over time, she will learn that wherever she goes or whatever decisions she makes, her mother is always there for her and will love her unconditionally no matter what the outcome is.

3. Strengthening the mother-daughter bond.

By making an unconditional commitment to a mother-daughter relationship, she will feel loved and strong. You can help her build self-confidence by teaching her that no matter what happens in life or whatever mistakes she may make, it is okay to ask for guidance and support from you.

As she grows older, your unconditional commitment to her will help her feel secure in any decisions she makes in life. She will know that you are always there for her and that you will support her through the good times and the bad.

4. Helping her find her inner strength.

By making an unconditional commitment to a mother-daughter relationship, your daughter will feel that she can seek help whenever she needs it.

She will feel free to talk to you and share anything that is on her mind. This is a good way for her to express any doubts or fears that may exist in her life.

She will find it easy to reach out and ask for your help when she needs it. This is the ultimate way to help build her self-confidence.

5. Helping her develop self-reliance.

By making an unconditional commitment to a mother-daughter relationship, she will learn the importance of being self-reliant as she grows older and develops into an adult. This is an excellent way to help your daughter grow into the strong, independent woman that she is meant to be.

She will learn that it is okay to look out for her own future and that she can depend on you no matter what decision she may make in life. This will teach her the importance of growing up and being able to take care of herself when her parents are no longer able to help her with any problems that may arise.

6. Helping her have compassion for others.

By making an unconditional commitment to a mother-daughter relationship, she will learn the importance of having compassion for others. She will be able to understand that people have different ways of thinking and acting. She will feel good when she is able to put herself in another person's shoes and understand where they are coming from.

She will learn that it is important not to judge a person before knowing their true motives. Your unconditional commitment to her as her mother will allow her to develop compassion for others no matter what their differences may be.

she will be able to understand people and what they are thinking. She can develop the ability to make the correct decision in any situation knowing that she has the guidance of her mother to help guide her along the way.

7. Helping her become responsible.

By making an unconditional commitment to a mother-daughter relationship, she will be able to feel confident and secure in the decision. She will learn that within her family, everyone cares for one another and can support each other through anything that may come their way.

This is an excellent way for your daughter to feel secure when she can look out for her future by being responsible for herself. Over time, she will begin to take charge of her own life and become confident in any decisions she makes in order to help others who may need any sort of support from her. This way you teach your daughter the importance of being self-reliant and taking responsibility for her own well-being.

8. Teach her that she is loved no matter what decision she makes.

By making an unconditional commitment to a mother-daughter relationship, you will be teaching her to be strong and independent. Teaching her that she can make mistakes and learn from them and encouraging her to never give up.

It is an excellent way to teach her the importance of being responsible for her own well-being. This is something that will take time, but over time you and your daughter will be able to build a solid relationship that will grow stronger as she becomes an adult. You can show her that no matter what choices she makes in life you will always be there for support and guidance, helping her make new decisions and not pushing her in a certain direction.

How to make a lifetime commitment and create an everlasting bond

Mothers and daughters have a very special relationship. It is a bond that will last forever. Like everything else in life, it takes work to make it stronger, but it can be done with a little effort and a lot of love. Most mothers want their daughters to feel as though they are loved and needed by their families, especially by them. They want to help their daughters grow into happy, healthy adults who feel confident about themselves no matter what happens in life or the choices they make.

The following are steps on how to make a lifetime commitment and create an everlasting bond:

Step 1: Let your own emotions guide you.

Before you can fully commit yourself to your daughter, you must first allow yourself to feel the emotions and the joy that comes with having a mother-daughter relationship.

If you want to make a lifelong commitment, then it is important for you to understand that you need to be emotionally available in your daughter's life. Show her that mistakes are a part of learning by being patient and understanding, but also be ready to step in when it happens.

You need to be consistent in your parenting expectations, as it helps your daughter feel secure and supported, so she can come to you with any concern she may have.

Step 2: Tell her how much she means to you.

Make sure you let your daughter know that you will always be there for her. Doing so will give her the courage to make decisions in life even if she knows that there may be some trouble along the way.

She can depend on you for anything and won't feel scared about making a mistake because she knows that you love her unconditionally.

Step 3: Learn to communicate with one another.

Daughters need to communicate with their mothers in order to build a strong relationship with them and develop into happy, confident women when they are older.

This is something that the two of you should do together. If your daughter is upset with you, get her to talk to you in order to make things better. Always listen to her and understand her, then make sure you tell her how much she means to you and that she can always depend on you for support.

Step 4: Be patient with one another.

Mothers and daughters are very close during childhood because they share a special bond with one another that no one else can ever understand unless they are a mother or a daughter themselves.

But this special bond cannot be maintained outside of the home unless you work together as mothers and daughters to make it strong. The most important thing that you can do for her is to be patient with her and give her plenty of time to grow into the woman she wants to become. This is something that takes a lot of time, but it will make your relationship stronger and your daughter more confident about herself.

Step 5: Keep an open mind.

If you want your daughter to feel loved and supported, then it's very important for you to keep an open mind about any decisions she makes in life.

Don't push her to make decisions that may not be the best for her. Try to understand what she wants in her life, but do not make any decisions for her if she does not agree with them. just show support and pride and guidance during the process of making her decisions.

Step 6: Make a lifetime commitment to your relationship and be completely devoted to each other, even if you don't agree.

Your mother-daughter relationship is going to grow stronger and stronger as time goes on. If you both want it to go as far as it can go or even further than that, then you must first make a lifetime commitment to one another.

Tell each other how much you love and cherish each other. Mother and daughter relationships are very special and should be treasured no matter what the circumstances are when they are put together.

You and your daughter have a unique relationship and both of you need to know that your mother-daughter relationship is special no matter what anyone else has to say about it. If you make a lifetime commitment to one another, then work together as mothers and daughters to make the best out of your relationship and make all your dreams come true.

Chapter 11

The Power of the Subconscious Mind in Raising a Daughter

R aising a daughter is undoubtedly a huge challenge, but it doesn't have to be overwhelming. In fact, the power of the subconscious mind can provide an invaluable tool in forming a special bond with your little girl and helping her to become a strong, independent, and capable woman.

By understanding how the subconscious mind works, parents can take steps to create an environment in which their daughter's personality can flourish and shape a mindset that will give her the courage to face whatever comes to her way with confidence. with the help of positive thoughts and self-empowerment, children can grow-up with a strong sense of self and a zest for life that will stay with them for years to come.

Every day, you are setting the emotional foundation for your daughter to be a young lady of good character. From the earliest moments of her life, you can plant seeds of love and care by being her first female role model. This is certainly easy to do when your daughter is just a baby, and you feel unconditional love towards her with every ounce of who you are. The power of the subconscious mind in raising a daughter begins with setting a foundation of love for your daughter.

Understanding the importance of working on a daughter's subconscious mind

Working on a daughter's subconscious mind is an essential part of raising a strong, resilient and successful daughter. It's important to understand that the subconscious mind holds powerful beliefs, traits and emotions that can manifest in her behavior and attitude.

By focusing on exposing your daughter to positive influences and helping her create an understanding of how her feelings, actions and decisions affect her life.

You can work on her subconscious mind to create a strong foundation for her future. This allows her to develop a healthy sense of self-worth and resilience, as well as identify bad habits and reframe them into positive thought patterns. Through this process, she'll be better prepared to face life's challenges and make smart choices.

Daughters are born with universal love and recognition of motherly instincts within them from the very beginning of their lives which are passed down from mother to daughter through genetics.

This deeply rooted subconscious trait is one of the most important factors in influencing your daughter's subconscious mind. It allows you to have a direct effect on how your daughter feels about herself and about the world around her.

The power of the subconscious mind in raising a daughter is the ability to create a supportive and nurturing environment that encourages success and resilience. It involves understanding the needs of your daughter and addressing them in a positive way. as well as setting a good example and teaching skills that help her reach her full potential.

Talking about things that really matter to both of you, will be remembered, and she will always draw on these memories when she feels overwhelmed or needs support. You set the emotional foundation for your daughter from her earliest years. The more time you spend with your daughter, talking about anything and everything, the more opportunities you will develop the power of love for your daughter's subconscious mind.

Once this foundation is established for your daughter's subconscious mind, you have already created a long-term relationship between you and her. Now all that's left is to keep building it over time to create a deep friendship where your primary concern is empowering both of you to be as wonderful as possible in life.

Assuring your daughter that she can confide in you with anything is another crucial step in developing a strong relationship with her. You want her to have the ability to come to you with her frustrations, fears, and insecurities.

To establish this, you need to plant the seeds of trust, water them with open communication, honesty, and positivity and let them grow to develop a strong everlasting foundation of mother-daughter love and friendship.

Teaching daughters to take the positive side of every conflict or problem in life

The subconscious mind in raising a daughter is designed to be a battlefield for you to fight for your daughter's highest potential. The way you do this is by teaching her how to use the power of her subconscious mind to overcome any challenge or adversity in life.

Teaching daughters to take the positive side of every conflict or problem in life is one of the most important subconscious parenting skills to learn in raising a daughter. It's an important part of helping them develop resilience and success. By teaching them to analyze and break down each situation into smaller pieces, they can take a more proactive and rational solution to the problem.

How to teach daughters to take the positive side of every conflict or problem in life?

Take time to listen to your daughter describe what she is struggling with in detail. Ask questions to help her see the positive aspects of her story and the positive side of the experience and be encouraged by it.

By seeing the good, it helps her realize that with the right mindset and effort, she can make the situation work for her. This type of attitude encourages her to learn from her mistakes and to continue pushing despite obstacles.

It also helps her develop problem-solving skills and critical thinking, which allow her to change her behavior and make more informed decisions. let her know that you are on her side by empathizing with how hard it must be for her. Don't try to judge or criticize anything.

When your daughter learns how to take the positive side of every situation in life, it will allow her to experience unconditional love and self-acceptance more deeply than most people do. Most people are taught to blame others for their feelings of shame, disappointment, and regret. They're not taught that they have a right to feel good about themselves, even though they may make a mistake or experience some difficulty in life.

It's also important for your daughter to learn how to accept the difficult situations in her life as part of her journey toward greater success and happiness. She doesn't have to be perfect to be acceptable. You want her to realize that she is perfect just the way she is and that there's no need for her to try so hard if she chooses not to go there at all.

Strategies for setting a positive subconscious mind for success in life

The way you raise your daughter's subconscious mind has a significant effect on how successful she will become. To help her become as successful as possible, it's important to focus on empowering her to feel good about herself, no matter what she's going through.

When your daughter feels good about herself, it makes her more capable of achieving great success in all areas of her life. It also makes it easier for her to believe that she deserves the best things in life and that there's no limit to what she can do or be.

"Whatever the mind can conceive and believe,
the mind can achieve"
(Napoleon Hills)

This positive mental attitude becomes part of who your daughter is and helps give her a greater sense of self-worth than if she had been raised with negative expectations and beliefs. The subconscious mind is more powerfully influenced by the belief system you raise your daughter with.

The following are strategies for setting a positive subconscious mind for success in life when raising a daughter:

1. Teach her to believe in herself. Most people are taught from a very young age that they are not good enough, or there's something wrong with them because they struggle with something during their lives. These beliefs and expectations keep them trapped in their challenges and struggles for the rest of their lives.

2. Teach her to value her mistakes and not fear them. Encourage her to use her mistakes as learning opportunities and to develop a growth mindset.

3. Facilitate positive conversations with her and highlight successful role models such as women in leadership positions to show her that anything is possible.

4. Provide her with plenty of opportunities to explore her passions and interests and talk to her about her dreams. Allow her to discover her strengths and weaknesses and encourage her to pursue what she loves.

5. Let her know that failure is part of life and that it is important to not let it sway her from her path. Instead, use failure as a learning lesson to help her become more resilient.

6. Recognize and applaud her successes, no matter how small. reiterate that focus and hard work often result in success.

7. Teach her to appreciate every success she accomplishes.
    As your daughter accomplishes different things in life, take time to celebrate her successes with her. create special memories together when she accomplishes something important.

8. Teach her that she deserves the best things in life.
    Your daughter's subconscious mind needs to be raised with a belief that she deserves the best, and she can have or be anything she wants if she puts efforts into it and never gives up.

Children who are raised to believe they deserve more often have the drive and passion to achieve great success in life. They understand that they have power over their own lives because they own what they've been given inside of them.

When you raise your daughter to believe she deserves the best things in life, it makes her more capable of stepping forward to her potential of greatness.

You want to raise your daughter's subconscious mind to help her make decisions and choices that will enable her to achieve success in life, no matter what. If the wrong beliefs are placed inside her subconscious mind during childhood, she will have a difficult time attracting what she wants because she doesn't believe that she deserves it.

When this happens, it makes it harder for your daughter to perceive reality for what it really is, because she has negative expectations about herself and other people.

When your daughter learns how to believe in herself and understands that she is a wonderful person despite past challenges and mistakes, she will feel more empowered to act toward her goals and dreams in life. She will also be able to reach new heights that were invisible before because she can see them now. This will allow her the freedom to choose her own path, no matter what challenges she encounters along the way.

Being a parent of a daughter who takes the positive side of every conflict or problem in life gives you an opportunity to help influence how successful they are by their subconscious mind.

Case study

The power of the subconscious mind isn't something that can be fully understood, but it can be harnessed to help improve your daughter's life. The following is one example of how a parent's influence over how their child perceives their life experiences can make a big difference in how they view themselves and the world.

Sandy is a successful professional and the proud mother of a little girls Sarah. Although sandy can provide her daughter with all of the material comforts and security she needs, she become increasingly concerned about

Sarah's lack of self-confidence, and school failures. She remembered that she was constantly criticizing and blaming Sarah for her bad choices and feedbacks because daily challenges in dealing with every situation. This judgment made Sarah believe and accept that she is not good enough to achieve any success.

After months of research, sandy discovers the power of subconscious mind and releases that she is the reason for her daughter's troubles.

To implement this method, sandy enrolls in a series of workshops and classes to learn about the power of the subconscious mind. She then sets to work on creating a positive and encouraging environment for her daughter at home.

Sandy focuses on using positive affirmations, positive reinforcement, visualizing success and focusing on Sarah's strengths.

She also invests time and energy into making Sarah's dreams and goals a reality. For instance, sandy works hard to find an after-school activity for Sarah that she enjoys and excels at. She also incorporates relaxation techniques such as meditation and yoga into Sarah's daily routine in order to help her daughter learn to calm her mind and practice self-control.

After months of consistency implementing the power of the subconscious into Sarah's daily life. Sandy sees an incredible transformation in her daughter. It took a lot of hard work on Sarah's part to overcome all the negative expectations put into her mind. She had to learn how to think more positively before she could ever become successful.

Within a span of time, Sarah has begun to believe in herself, and her capabilities. She became successful when she learned how to accept and love herself. She also learned how to block the past negative experiences from distorting her view of who she was in the present, which enabled her to move forward with a newfound sense of optimism and enthusiasm.

By using the power of the subconscious mind confidently and deliberately, sandy was able to create a positive and encouraging environment in which her daughter has been able to blossom and thrive.

The power of the subconscious mind can be used to turn your daughter's thoughts around to help her see that she doesn't need the negative beliefs in her subconscious mind to stop them from being successful.

You want your daughter's subconscious mind to believe that she is a wonderful person who deserves good things in life, no matter what has happened in her past experiences with disappointments and failures.

When your daughter believes she is a wonderful person and can create the positive results, she will be more likely to take action toward her goals and dreams in life. She'll also feel better about herself because she knows she has the power to manifest any success she wants in life if she so chooses.

As a parent of your daughter, it's important for you to understand and accept yourself no matter how much you change over the years or what challenges you encounter along the way. No matter where you are now, who you are, or how far you've come, there will always be new experiences, deals, and challenges around you.

It would be best if you kept moving because the only way to succeed is to enjoy the journey and look forward to what you'll find along the way. Your daughter needs to understand that nothing is permanent in her life, and there will be new challenges and experiences for her as she continues down her path.

The positive side of every experience or problem your daughter faces allow you to have power over how successful she becomes during her lifetime. You need to understand how much power you have over your daughter's dreams and goals in life.

Your daughter's subconscious mind will always try to push forward her negative beliefs about herself and the world around her. When you teach your daughter to replace her negative views with positive ones, she can see life differently than others and gain a new perspective on anything she encounters.

By following these steps, the mother in this case study was able to build a strong, healthy relationship with her daughter. She created an everlasting bond that lasted a lifetime, and the two of them remained best friends even as the daughter grew up and became an adult.

Conclusion

The journey continues...

A healthy mother-daughter relationship is an ongoing process of building trust, respect, and communication. it is a life-long connection that is nurtured by nurturing one another's aspirations, encouraging each other's dreams, and teaching each other about the importance of mistakes and failure.

With love and understanding, a mother-daughter relationship can develop into a secure and rewarding friendship that will last a lifetime.

The recipe for a life-long friendship between a mother and daughter is one that takes time and effort to perfect. by putting trust in each other, communicating openly, and showing respect and understanding, you can begin to create an unbreakable bond.

With these three ingredients, it's possible to mix in moments of fun and laughter to create a special relationship that will last a lifetime.

As a daughter grows up and steps out into the world, it's the mother's job to be a loving and supportive friend who can guide her child. mothers should encourage daughters to try new things, learn from their mistakes, and to think of the world around them in new exciting ways. Through conversations and activities, they can learn to be independent while still being able to rely on each other.

By setting boundaries and listening to one another, a mother and daughter can create a mutual understanding. Through communication and understanding, a daughter can learn to become patient, kind, and forgiving.

Mothers should show love and acceptance, even during periods of disagreement.

As a daughter continues to bloom, she will learn how to nurture her own relationship with her friends and family. Mothers should never deny their daughters the opportunity to express themselves and take responsibility for their decisions.

With freedom and responsibility comes strength, resilience, and a newfound sense of love and appreciation.

Finally, a mother-daughter relationship should be filled with memories that are meaningful and lasting. Whenever possible, try to create memories together, such as movie nights, picnics, museum visits, and hikes. These moments will help to build treasured bonds and create a rock-solid foundation for a life-long friendship between a mother and daughter.

The recipe for a life-long friendship between a mother and daughter can take many forms and will look different for every family. Motherhood is never easy. It is the toughest role in a woman's life, and there are moments when the experience makes an average woman feel like they are just not going to make it. But it is by no means possible.

All mothers need to be open-minded and listen, re-establishing a bond with their daughters, no matter how much time passes, you will always be the first and only love of your daughter's life.

Keep an open mind that your daughter might be going through a rebellious stage in her life; therefore, it is best not to impose certain rules which are too old-fashioned or outdated that can cause conflicts between both of you.

When it comes right down, it is vital that the mother's intentions are only good – she wants only what is best for her daughter regardless of what society thinks or says regarding the subject.

The mother needs to understand that it is all right for her not to always be the perfect parent. All parents will have days where things get out of control. They can take time to settle.

Allow your daughter the freedom she needs to develop in the direction she chooses. Remember that this is a process she will go through during her life, so enjoy and embrace it because it is going to be one of the hardest experiences of your life. Get used to it, accept it, and allow yourself the chance for growth and learning too.

The End.

Dear reader! Thank you for reading, I hope you have enjoyed my book, if you have, I would be so grateful if you could share your thoughts about it by leaving an honest book review on Amazon... Your feedback will be much appreciated.

Thank you very much in advance.

Made in the USA
Monee, IL
13 September 2023